" if only you knew
the magnificence of the 3, 6 and 9,
then you would have the key to the universe "

- Nikola Tesla

Let's manifest, baby

Are you ready to change your life in the next 21 days? It may sound extreme but with the 3-6-9 manifestation method you can do just that. The 3-6-9 manifestation method is an extremely powerful technique that breaks manifestation down in an easy structure.

Here's how it works:
First, pick what it is that you want to manifest, a promotion, for example. Each morning, shortly after waking up, write down that manifestation three times. In the afternoon, write it down six more times. Finally, at night, write it down nine times.

To make the 3-6-9 manifestation technique even more powerful ensure you:
- Whilst writing, try to believe you already have what you're trying to manifest - allow yourself to envision it as real.
- The way you word your manifestation is important. Phrase your statement in present tense, as though you already have the thing you're manifesting. If you're manifesting a promotion, you could use: "I am so grateful and inspired by this promotion I have received at work".
- Repetition and routine is key - follow this journal everyday and make it a habit.

Why 3,6 and 9?

The numerology of these numbers is significant. In the practice, the number three directly connects us to the universe or the source, six represents the strength we have within ourselves, and nine helps us to move on from the past and releases any self-doubt we have. Frequency is an important factor in manifestation practices, and tapping into these numbers (divine or not) might just help turn your wishes into reality. Whilst some people report seeing results the next day, 21 days are generally suggested for best results.

Raising your frequency is key in manifestation and can really speed things up. Crystals, frequency music and incense are all powerful tools that can be used alongside this journal. For example; when manifesting love you could use a Rose Quartz crystal, listen to 528 Hz music and burn rose incense. For money and wealth manifestations you could use a Citrine crystal, play 183.58 Hz music and burn Frankincense. You do not have to do all of these things at once, but incorporating even one extra tool can make a big difference.

In this journal you will find space for 21 days worth of 3-6-9 manifestation and daily journaling prompts to encourage positive thoughts. I have also included 4 lists of positive affirmations for you to repeat daily and a scripting activity to finish with. Now, are you ready to start? Take a deep breath and confidently repeat the mantra on the following page.

I RELEASE MY LIMITING BELIEFS

I RELEASE THOSE RELATIONSHIPS THAT NO LONGER SERVE MY HIGHER GOOD

I RELEASE ALL OBSTACLES TO MY PATH

I RELEASE PAIN AND SUFFERING AS A MEANS TO GROWTH

I RELEASE ALL THAT WHICH IS NO LONGER IN ALIGNMENT WITH MY HIGHEST SELF FOR THE GREATEST GOOD

AFFIRMATIONS TO ATTRACT
LOVE

1. I am aligned with love.
2. I am constantly surrounded by love.
3. I radiate unconditional love.
4. I receive love in abundance.
5. Everything I do aligns with the vibration of love.
6. I love myself.
7. I am grateful for the abundance of love in my life.
8. Every cell in my body vibrates with love.
9. I am love.
10. My heart is open to give and receive love.
11. I welcome love into my life.
12. I spread love to those around me and it returns to me in abundance.
13. I am open to love.
14. My heart radiates love to those around me.
15. Love is on its way to me.

AFFIRMATIONS TO ATTRACT
MONEY

1. Money flows easily to me.
2. I am a money magnet.
3. I am in harmony with the energy of money.
4. I am energy. Money is energy.
5. Money always finds its way to me.
6. I am aligned with the energy of wealth and abundance.
7. The more money I spend, the more money I have and receive.
8. I am financially free.
9. I make money easily.
10. I release all resistance to attracting money.
11. I love money because money loves me.
12. I always have enough money.
13. I accept and receive unexpected money.
14. I never worry about money.

AFFIRMATIONS TO ATTRACT
SUCCESS

1. I am successful.
2. I have the power to create all the success and prosperity I desire.
3. I am a magnet for success.
4. My mind is a magnet for success.
5. My potential to succeed is infinite.
6. The universe is filled with endless opportunities.
7. I am worthy of all the success I desire.
8. I can achieve greatness.
9. I find it easy to succeed in everything that I do.
10. I am highly motivated and productive.
11. Everything always works out for me.
12. I am grateful for all my success.
13. My goals and dreams always come true.
14. I am the architect of my life.
15. I continuously push myself to learn and develop.

AFFIRMATIONS TO ATTRACT
HEALTH

1. I am healthy and full of energy.
2. Healthy, vibrant energy flows through my body naturally.
3. I easily attract good and positive energy to mind, body, and soul.
4. The Universe helps me achieve beautiful levels of health and wellness.
5. I enjoy existing in a natural state of well-being.
6. I welcome positive and healthy energy with open arms.
7. Every day is an opportunity to enjoy new levels of energy and well-being.
8. I choose to let my natural, glorious, and healthy energy shine.
9. It comes naturally for me to feel good and healthy.
10. I am a magnet for healthy, uplifting, and empowering energy.

DAY 1

MORNING

1. _____
2. _____
3. _____

AFTERNOON

1. _____
2. _____
3. _____
4. _____
5. _____
6. _____

EVENING

1. _____
2. _____
3. _____
4. _____
5. _____
6. _____
7. _____
8. _____
9. _____

3 things I am grateful for:
_____
_____
_____

GRATITUDE

3 people I am grateful for:
_____
_____
_____

DAY 2

MORNING

1. _____
2. _____
3. _____

AFTERNOON

1. _____
2. _____
3. _____
4. _____
5. _____
6. _____

EVENING

1. _____
2. _____
3. _____
4. _____
5. _____
6. _____
7. _____
8. _____
9. _____

3 things I love about my appearance:
_____
_____
_____

SELF-LOVE

3 positive words to describe me:

_____

_____

_____

DAY 3

MORNING

1. _____
2. _____
3. _____

AFTERNOON

1. _____
2. _____
3. _____
4. _____
5. _____
6. _____

EVENING

1. _____
2. _____
3. _____
4. _____
5. _____
6. _____
7. _____
8. _____
9. _____

3 things that make me laugh:
_____
_____
_____

HAPPINESS

3 films that make me happy:
_____
_____
_____

DAY 4

MORNING

1. _____
2. _____
3. _____

AFTERNOON

1. _____
2. _____
3. _____
4. _____
5. _____
6. _____

EVENING

1. _____
2. _____
3. _____
4. _____
5. _____
6. _____
7. _____
8. _____
9. _____

3 things I am looking forward to:

_____
_____
_____

POSITIVITY

3 things I have overcome:

_____
_____
_____

DAY 5

MORNING
1. _____
2. _____
3. _____

AFTERNOON
1. _____
2. _____
3. _____
4. _____
5. _____
6. _____

EVENING
1. _____
2. _____
3. _____
4. _____
5. _____
6. _____
7. _____
8. _____
9. _____

3 places I have visited and loved:

_____
_____
_____

ADVENTURE

3 places I would love to visit:

_____

_____

_____

DAY 6

MORNING

1. _____
2. _____
3. _____

AFTERNOON

1. _____
2. _____
3. _____
4. _____
5. _____
6. _____

EVENING

1. _____
2. _____
3. _____
4. _____
5. _____
6. _____
7. _____
8. _____
9. _____

3 things I have achieved:
_____
_____
_____

SUCCESS

3 things I would like to achieve:
_____
_____
_____

DAY 7

MORNING

1. _____
2. _____
3. _____

AFTERNOON

1. _____
2. _____
3. _____
4. _____
5. _____
6. _____

EVENING

1. _____
2. _____
3. _____
4. _____
5. _____
6. _____
7. _____
8. _____
9. _____

3 things I do to stay healthy:
_____
_____
_____

HEALTH

3 things I would like to try to improve my health:
_____
_____
_____

DAY 8

MORNING
1. _____
2. _____
3. _____

AFTERNOON
1. _____
2. _____
3. _____
4. _____
5. _____
6. _____

EVENING
1. _____
2. _____
3. _____
4. _____
5. _____
6. _____
7. _____
8. _____
9. _____

3 things I want to feel today:

_____
_____
_____

FEELINGS

3 things I can do that will support me in feeling those things:

_____

_____

_____

DAY 9

MORNING

1. _____
2. _____
3. _____

AFTERNOON

1. _____
2. _____
3. _____
4. _____
5. _____
6. _____

EVENING

1. _____
2. _____
3. _____
4. _____
5. _____
6. _____
7. _____
8. _____
9. _____

3 smells that bring back happy memories:

_____
_____
_____

SENSES

3 sounds that bring back happy memories:

_____
_____
_____

DAY 10

MORNING

1. _____
2. _____
3. _____

AFTERNOON

1. _____
2. _____
3. _____
4. _____
5. _____
6. _____

EVENING

1. _____
2. _____
3. _____
4. _____
5. _____
6. _____
7. _____
8. _____
9. _____

3 of my favourite flowers:

_____
_____
_____

NATURE

3 of my favourite animals:

_____

_____

_____

DAY 11

MORNING
1. _____
2. _____
3. _____

AFTERNOON
1. _____
2. _____
3. _____
4. _____
5. _____
6. _____

EVENING
1. _____
2. _____
3. _____
4. _____
5. _____
6. _____
7. _____
8. _____
9. _____

3 things I do to relax:
_____
_____
_____

RELAXATION

Describe a time you felt at peace:
_____
_____
_____

DAY 12

MORNING

1. _____
2. _____
3. _____

AFTERNOON

1. _____
2. _____
3. _____
4. _____
5. _____
6. _____

EVENING

1. _____
2. _____
3. _____
4. _____
5. _____
6. _____
7. _____
8. _____
9. _____

3 things that make me feel good:
_____
_____
_____

SELF-CARE

3 things I can do today to show myself self-care:
_____
_____
_____

DAY 13

MORNING

1. _____
2. _____
3. _____

AFTERNOON

1. _____
2. _____
3. _____
4. _____
5. _____
6. _____

EVENING

1. _____
2. _____
3. _____
4. _____
5. _____
6. _____
7. _____
8. _____
9. _____

An opportunity I'm grateful for:
_____
_____
_____

GRATITUDE

A freedom I'm grateful for:
_____
_____
_____

DAY 14

MORNING

1. _____
2. _____
3. _____

AFTERNOON

1. _____
2. _____
3. _____
4. _____
5. _____
6. _____

EVENING

1. _____
2. _____
3. _____
4. _____
5. _____
6. _____
7. _____
8. _____
9. _____

3 things I love to watch on TV:

_____
_____
_____

ENTERTAINMENT

3 activities I enjoy:

_____
_____
_____

DAY 15

MORNING

1. _____
2. _____
3. _____

AFTERNOON

1. _____
2. _____
3. _____
4. _____
5. _____
6. _____

EVENING

1. _____
2. _____
3. _____
4. _____
5. _____
6. _____
7. _____
8. _____
9. _____

3 songs I love the lyrics of:
_____
_____
_____

MUSIC

3 songs that make me smile:
_____
_____
_____

DAY 16

MORNING

1. _____
2. _____
3. _____

AFTERNOON

1. _____
2. _____
3. _____
4. _____
5. _____
6. _____

EVENING

1. _____
2. _____
3. _____
4. _____
5. _____
6. _____
7. _____
8. _____
9. _____

3 things that make me feel peaceful:
_____
_____
_____

FEELINGS

3 things that make me feel excited:
_____
_____
_____

DAY 17

MORNING

1. _____
2. _____
3. _____

AFTERNOON

1. _____
2. _____
3. _____
4. _____
5. _____
6. _____

EVENING

1. _____
2. _____
3. _____
4. _____
5. _____
6. _____
7. _____
8. _____
9. _____

3 things I like about where I live:
_____
_____
_____

POSITIVITY

My favourite positivity quote:
_____

_____

_____

DAY 18

MORNING

1. _____
2. _____
3. _____

AFTERNOON

1. _____
2. _____
3. _____
4. _____
5. _____
6. _____

EVENING

1. _____
2. _____
3. _____
4. _____
5. _____
6. _____
7. _____
8. _____
9. _____

3 people who mean the most to me:
_____
_____
_____

PEOPLE

3 people that are always kind to me:
_____
_____
_____

DAY 19

MORNING

1. _____
2. _____
3. _____

AFTERNOON

1. _____
2. _____
3. _____
4. _____
5. _____
6. _____

EVENING

1. _____
2. _____
3. _____
4. _____
5. _____
6. _____
7. _____
8. _____
9. _____

3 of my favourite snacks:

_____
_____
_____

NUTRITION

3 of my favourite things to cook:

_____
_____
_____

DAY 20

MORNING

1. _____
2. _____
3. _____

AFTERNOON

1. _____
2. _____
3. _____
4. _____
5. _____
6. _____

EVENING

1. _____
2. _____
3. _____
4. _____
5. _____
6. _____
7. _____
8. _____
9. _____

My favourite part of the day:
_____
_____
_____

HAPPINESS

My favourite meal time:

_____

_____

_____

DAY 21

MORNING

1. _____
2. _____
3. _____

AFTERNOON

1. _____
2. _____
3. _____
4. _____
5. _____
6. _____

EVENING

1. _____
2. _____
3. _____
4. _____
5. _____
6. _____
7. _____
8. _____
9. _____

My favourite season, and why:
_____
_____
_____

SEASONS

A tradition I look forward to every year:
_____
_____
_____

SCRIPTING ACTIVITY
How To Script Your Dream Life Into Existence

1. Get very specific about what it is that you want but ensure that you believe it.

2. Use the space on the next page to write down what you want, but remember to use present or past tense, indicating that you have already manifested it.

3. Feel the feelings you'd feel if you had it already. You can do this by imagining the sounds, the smells, the actual visuals of how it would feel to have the thing that you are manifesting.

4. Finish your scripting entry by expressing a lot of gratitude to the universe for delivering your blessing in a divinely timed manner.

5. Close the journal and know that it is done. Do not obsess over when or how you will receive the blessing, just know that you have scripted it, it is yours and you will soon see it in your physical reality.

Let's stay in touch!

I love to chat! Follow me over on Instagram and keep up with my new releases.
@ievaremeikyte

Printed in Great Britain
by Amazon